SOUTHERN SAYIN'S
FOR
YANKEES
AND OTHER IMMIGRANTS

Compiled and Cartooned
by
Bill Dwyer

EF YOU WANTS TO SEE HOW MUCH FOLKS IS
GWINE TO MISS YOU, JEST STICK YOUR
FINGER IN THE POND AND PULL IT OUT
THEN LOOK AT THE HOLE.
       Mississippi Negro

"The Post Card & Souvenir People" ™

2511 South Tryon Street • Charlotte, NC 28203
(704) 333-5143 • Fax: (704) 333-5148 • Toll Free Fax: (800) 204-4910
Website: www.aps-1.com • E-mail: aps@aps-1.com

Regional Locations:

| Atlanta, GA | (770) 428-2669 | Myrtle Beach, SC | (910) 575-6660 |
| Gatlinburg, TN | (865) 436-7831 | Outer Banks, NC | (252) 449-0400 |

© 2004 Aerial Photography Services, Inc.

ISBN 0-936672-30-7

No part of this book may be reproduced or transmitted in any form or by any means without express written permission from Aerial Photography Services, Inc.

FUST—LET'S GET YOU-ALL STRAIGHTENED OUT!

YOU-ALL, YA'LL, pronoun — Usually said when addressing two or more persons or, sometimes one person as representing another or others. "You-all and we-all, you-uns and we-uns" invariably refer to more than one individual, i.e. "How you-all this morning? —— Where ya'll going? —— I'm right proud to know you-all thought to come. —— See you all in church." It is commonly alleged and believed in the North that in some parts of the South YOU-ALL (with the accent on the YOU) is frequently used with a singular meaning. On the other hand, most Southerners emphatically, not to say indignantly, deny that this expression is ever employed in the South with reference to a single individual. They assert that they always have in mind some other person or persons in addition to the one they are addressing.

YOU-ALL, the singular —— Contrary to what is said by some, you-all often means one person and is a very common greeting. "Good Morning! How ya'all this morning?" or "Where are you-all going this morning?" - not withstanding that you are quite alone. Other examples of the singular "No, I don't like you-all in that dress." — "You-all know about that restaurant?" —— "You-all one of those Dwyers?"

YOU-ALLS, pronoun, plural —— "You-alls come by and see us! — "What are you-alls going to do next?"

YOU-ALL'S, adjective, your — "Let's go over to ya'll's house." — "'I saw you-all's car in town." — "We were just coming over to you-all's."

·PROUD·

PROUD, adj.; GLAD, HAPPY, PLEASED — A word used extensively throughout the South in everyday speech. —— "I am mighty proud to meet you. —— Proud to see you looking so well. — I'll bet your mother was proud to see you. — I'm right proud you-all thought to come. — I'm just proud of a chance to help."

PROUD, adj.; FINE, LAUDABLE, SELF-RESPECTING —– "Then he did a proud thing."

To the Southerner .. 'PROUD' ("too proud to fight") has a different meaning. A Southerner will say, "I'm too proud to do it." - A Northerner would say, "My self-respect will not allow it." It is in that sense that the Southerner uses the word 'proud.'

·RECKON·

RECKON — To suppose, think, guess, believe; also, calculate, affirm, presume, expect, know, imagine, assume: — Usually parenthetically in "I RECKON." The Southerner most often means "I guess" — I reckon a storm is coming. — Well, I reckon so. — T'ain't powerful long to dinner, I reckon. — Reckon he'll come? — I reckon hit don't make no difference. — I reckon he'll come tomorrow. — I reckon city folks have to live same as anyone else.

RECKON? — Do you suppose?

RECKON, as in "I reckon" means Yes! - "Can you cash this check for me?" — "I reckon." ..... "You cold, son?" — "I reckon."

RECKON, as in questions equivalent to (Do you) know?: — Reckon who he is? — Reckon what time it is? — Reckon how he does that? — Reckon where paw is at?

RECKON — To wonder: — Reckon what the old man wants? - Now (I) reckon what he ever did that fer? — I reckon how many that car will hold? And so on.

·POWERFUL·

POWERFUL, adj., CONSIDER, IMMENSE —— Can be and often substituted by RIGHT SMART. Used in everyday speech by a large number, of Southerners.

Frequently non-Southern Americans are amused upon hearing the Southerner use the word POWERFUL; — "I'm powerful glad to see you. — I'm powerful tired. —— I'm powerful hungry. — His tractor is going powerful slow. —— He is powerful thin. — It does get powerful cold in the mountains. — He was powerful sot on going. — Powerful lucky. Powerful weak." And so on.

POWERFULLY, adverb, DEEPLY —— "A-studying and musin' powerfully."

UNCLE or ONCLE — AUNT or AUNTY —— In the South these are kindly or familiar titles, especially a common designation for any elderly man or woman. An outsider called "Uncle" can be assured he has been accepted by the townsfolk.

SOUTHERN SAYIN'S

GINGHAM PRETTY - Demure and innocent.

DOESN'T KNOW NITS FROM NOODLES - Stupid.

EATIN' HIGH ON THE HOG - Prosperous.

COME TO FETCH FIRE - To come and leave at once.

MASH THE LIGHT BUTTON - To push on or off.

DON'T YOU BACK-JAW ME - Talk back.

BLACKBERRY WINTER - Cold weather in the spring when blackberries are in bloom.

SAND IN MY SHOES - Can't escape from Florida.

A MULLET BLOW - Wind from the Northeast causing jumping mullet to school.

CHAWED UP, HEAD TO FOOT - Embarrassed.

SOUTHERN SAYIN'S

THET PIG'S SNOUT WAS SO LONG HE COULD STICK IT THROUGH A FENCE KNOTHOLE AND EAT THE GUTS OUT OF A PUMPKIN.

SHUT YOUR BUG GAP - Your mouth.

EVERYBODY TAKE AND RAKE - Invitation to begin eating.

GO TO THE BRIDGE WITH (one) - To befriend, support, stand by.

IT'S A FALLACY YOU'LL PAY FOR - A mistake or error.

SNOW or MUD IS SHOE-MOUTH DEEP - Up to the shoe-mouth or tongue of the shoe.

"WHERE YA PREACHIN'?" - Said to a man who is all dressed up.

DON'T COME BACK TO ME AFTER YOUR TARRYHOOTIN - To chase around, unfaithful.

I'M CARRYIN' A PET ON MY NOSE - Boil, sore, wart.

LISTEN TO THEM JIZZWITCHES - Katydids.

HOW'S IT GOING? - OKEEFENOKEE! - Substitute for "okay."

THAT WAS A HELLACIOUS WIND - Severe.

PALMETTO JUMPERS - (Georgia/Florida) - Cattle left to range without attention.

YOU'VE GOT A POCOSIN BRAIN - Swamp, low marsh land.

SANITARY STEP-ASIDE - Wall urinal.

WE HAVE THE BEST 'FRAID HOLE AROUND - A cave for refuge from storms.

YOU SLAB-SIDED GALLOOT - Tall and lank, sometimes meaning fat.

KNOCKED or SLAPPED, SKYWINDING - Helpless, senseless.

PRICES HAVE GONE A-SKYHOOTING - HER SKIRT WENT A-SKYHOOTING OVER HER NECK - Up.

WATCHIN' HIS BEES OR WAITING FOR HIS BEES TO SWARM - Euphemisms for expecting a baby.

HEM THE BEAR - To corner or put a person in a tight position.

DEVIL'S KITCHEN - Reference by women to a man's still-house.

DON'T JOREE ME - To make fun of.

SOUTHERN SAYIN'S

YOU'RE NOT JUST WHISTLING DIXIE - You are double correct! Right!

IT WAS A GOOSEDOWNER - cloudburst

THEY HAVE A GENERATION OF CHILDREN - A large family.

ALWAYS FUZZED-UP - Excited, disturbed.

"HOW ARE THEY BITING?" - "LIKE SMOKED MULLET!" (not at all)

SHE HAS LEGS LIKE A POJO - Long and skinny, like a heron, crane.

SHE LOVED TO FINGER HIS DRAKE'S TAIL - A tuft of hair at the back of the head.

LIMP AS A DISHRAG.

HIS TONGUE IS LONG ENOUGH TO CUT HIS THROAT.

SOUTHERN SAYIN'S

CAN TONGUE TOMATERS OFF THE VINE - Talkative.

TOMATOES - 'maters, tomaters, tomaties, tomattersus.

KEEP YOUR DAUBERS UP - Keep up your courage.

CAN TALK UP A TOW SACK - To fill a sack with foolish talk or nonsense.

HE PULLED UP A PULPIT - Said of anyone who carried on a lengthy conversation.

I'LL BE THERE IN A BREATH - In a moment.

DON'T YOU THROW A HISSY 'ROUND HERE - A fit of anger.

UPPITIES - Metropolitan tourists.

SUMMER/WINTER PEOPLE - Tourists, not year-around residents.

COMERS AND GOERS - Tourists.

TOURISTERS - Tourists.

THAT'S A AWFUL WOOLY-HEAD - Impassable thicket of laurel or rhododendron.

MAD AS FIRE. —— COLD AS BLUE FLUGINS.

SOUTHERN SAYIN'S

SNOWING LIKE WATER POURING OUT OF A BUCKET.

HEART BIG AS A COOT GIZZARD - A bird said to be all gizzard.

NEVER SAID PEA TURKEY - Never gave an invitation or offered information.

HE'S GOT THE RAISIN' OF A HOG - Rearing, manners, breeding.

HOW'D YOU LIKE TO GET EMBRANGLED WITH MY FISTES - Entangled with.

AGGER-PERVOKIN' OL' BUZZARD - Exasperating old man.

HE'S GOT THE HOOKWORM HUSTLE - Slow.

A HEN-PLUMP WOMAN - Fat.

GO BACK TO THE OVEN - Implies a person is "half-baked", not normal.

SOUTHERN SAYIN'S

I'LL SEE HIM DEEP IN HELL AS A PIGEON CAN FLY IN A WEEK.

HONGRY AS A LI'L OL' BUG IN A TATER PATCH.

ANGEL WINGS WON'T STOP HIS DEVIL-MINTING - Stop his misbehaving.

THEIR HEADS ARE INTO HARD TIMES - Financial difficulties.

AIN'T BIGGER'N A CRICKET, MUCH. - Small.

I SAW A COTTON-WHITE YESTERDAY - A grey fox that is sort of albino.

I'LL SPEW THE LANDSCAPE WITH YOU - Scatter, strew, cover.

"HOW ARE YOU TODAY?" - "ENJOYIN' POOR HEALTH, THANKEE!"

PAW'S TAKIN' TO PUNIN' AROUND - To act sick, dull.

THAT LAW-MAN'S A COLD TRAILER - Can pick up clues long forgotten or hidden.

PAW MADE A MISLICK AND CUT HIS FOOT - A false or awkward blow.

SOUTHERN SAYIN'S

IT'S JAYBIRD JABBER - Woman talk, gossip.

A-FLUTIN' AN' A-FLYIN' - Moving about in grand style.

TIGHT AS A TICK - Intoxicated.

NEVER MOVED AN EYEWINKER - Brave, never flinched.

MAD AS A HORNET - Mad as you can get.

A-GROWED TO THE CHAIR - Refuses to get up and move about.

GRINS LIKE A BAKED 'POSSUM.

NERVOUS AS A LONG-TAILED CAT IN A ROOMFULL OF ROCKING CHAIRS.

WENT SOUR ON ME - Turned out bad.

RUNNIN' 'ROUND LIKE A JUNEBUG ON A HOT GRIDDLE.

SOUTHERN SAYIN'S

IT'S A SIZZLE-SOZZLE - Gentle, steady rain.

SO LOW YOU HAVE TO REACH UP TO TOUCH BOTTOM.

MAD 'NUFF TO BITE A SPIKE-NAIL IN TWO.

I'LL TURN IT OVER AN' TICKLE IT FIRST - To think about an idea, to toy with it.

CUT MUD FER HOME - Left in a hurry.

HELD TOGETHER WITH FLOUR PASTE - A person who is easily upset or angered.

SOUR AS A PELICAN'S BREATH.

A LI'L OL' PEACH-FUZZY - Young child, below teenage.

PUT GREASE IN YER PAN, YER FISH IS BURNING - You are incorrect, lying, tell the truth!

HAPPY AS A STRAWBERRY COOTER - Turtle eating wild strawberries.

CROOKED AS A WORM ON A HOOK.

JUMPY (PEART) AS A CRICKET.

AIN'T MUCH - Not very well.

LIKE A BUG ARGUING WITH A CHICKEN.

YOU'RE BORROWING TROUBLE.

BEEN PONDERIN' SO HARD, AIN'T HAD TIME TO THINK.

EVERGLOM IS SO PRETTY - Evening twilight.

NERVOUS AS A FIDDLER - Fiddler crab.

NAKED AS A PARCHED PINDER - Roasted peanut.

HEAD FULL OF NOTIONS.

MAD AS A PUFFED TOAD-FROG.

MAD AS A SETTIN' HEN.

DRUNK AS A BOILED OWL.

FAST AS SNYDER'S HOUSE CAT.

NAKED AS A JAYBIRD.

SOUTHERN SAYIN'S

GO ON, TAKE THE RAG OFF - Stop pretending.

HE'S A HE-HUCKLEBERRY MAN - Large, strong, a huckleberry twice ordinary size.

IN LOW COTTON - feeling of depression.

A HEAP OF STIRRING AND NO BISCUITS - A lot of action, no results.

SPLIT THE QUILT - To separate, divorce

DRUNK AS A COOT.

SLIPPERY AS PIG SALVE - lard

ON THE DOWN GO - declining health

JOE IT ALONG - To move slowly.

A FUDDLE FUSSER - To fuss over something trivial.

SOUTHERN SAYIN'S

TO TRANSPORT - The countryman may LUG, TOTE, SHOULDER, HEFT or CARRY a parcel. These expressions are used in various sections of the South.

HIS TRUCK AIN'T GOT THE NOVEL WORE OFF YET - Newness.

THERE'S ISLANTS OFF THE COAST - Islands.

THAT MAN'S A JENNY - A man busied with the affairs of women.

NOISY AS A JARFLY - Cicada.

HE'S A-PRANKIN' WITH HIS CAR - To experiment, manipulate.

HE'S BEEN KEEPING HER UP FOR YEARS - To keep a mistress.

DON'T CARE A HATE - Small amount, bit.

HER HOUSE IS ALWAYS IN A MOMMICK - A mess, disorder.

YOU SHOULD MEET MY NEAR-BYS - My neighbors.

WHAT AN ONDOING - A pelting rain.

I DRINK MY WHISKEY REVEREND - Strong, not diluted.

SOUTHERN SAYIN'S

HIT WAS SO WET, PAW WAS SHOOTIN' WILD DUCKS IN THE PARLOR!

FULL OF TURKEY DREAMS - Daydreams.

CONTRARIOUS AS A SET DOWN JACKASS.

CAT-A-GOGLIN DRUNK - stumbling sideways

JUMPED THE BROOM - To get married

HEAD FULL OF STUMP WATER - Dumb.

HAPPY AS A DEAD PIG IN THE SUNSHINE.

BEAT THE MOSS OUT OF - Similar to beat the stuffing out of.

MOUTH CLUTTERED WITH TROUBLE - Asking for trouble.

A SHOE SCORPION - Sneaky, not to be trusted.

PASSING WORDS - Quarreling.

SOUTHERN SAYIN'S

LIKE A POKE-EASY MULE - Lazy, slow person.

BUNG YOUR MOUTH - Shut your mouth.

THINGS HAVE GONE AGLEY - askew, awry

GIVEN TO THE BALKS - sulking

IT WAS A FENCE LIFTER - rainstorm

AT YARNS END - Wits end, exasperated.

I AIN'T WORKING, JEST SPUDDIN' 'ROUND - To idle, loiter.

WEARS A HALF-MOON SMILE - Insincere.

I HAVE AN ACHIN' IN MY PRAYER BONES - In my knees.

I'M PLUMB WORRIED OUT - Wearied, tired.

WE'LL GET ALONG FINE IF HE'LL TOTE FAIR - Play fair, act or deal fairly.

TAKE THE STUDS - Become stubborn.

YOU ALWAYS UGLY MY FRIENDS OUTEN THE HOUSE - Drive out by words.

JAW LEAKS WATER - Drooling.

HE MADE A STRAIGHT COAT TAIL - Frightened, man running.

HAS MORE KINNERY THAN A RABBIT - Relatives, kindred.

DON'T TRY TO CUTE ME - Flatter.

YOU'RE A SOUR GRAPE TO ME - Enemy.

HE'S ALWAYS FIGGERIN' HOW TO CUT A RUSTY - To show off.

HE USES SWEET-ANNY WORMS TO CATCH CATFISH - Worms dipped in the anise herb.

DON'T TRY TO OUTDUGAN ME - To circumvent by questionable means.

I WAS THE FIRST TO RAISE IT IN CHURCH - To start the singing.

HE'D HOLD A FISH UNDER WATER TO DROWN IT - Stupid, dumb.

HOOZLE, HOOT - A drink of liquor.

I'LL HAVE SOME OF THOSE MYSTYDINES - Muscadine grapes.

A SNIBBLING DAY - Dark, cloudy, rainy.

SHE STARTED THE TUNE TOO SHALLER - Too high as to pitch.

SHO'- NUFF - Genuine, real, regular.

HE'S SO RAVEN 'BOUT HER HE CAN'T SLEEP NIGHTS - Enthusiastic, excited.

I JEST SELL OUT WHEN HE SHOWS UP - To leave quickly.

STOOD THERE AND KERFLUMMUXED THE JUDGE - Confused, to bewilder.

HE RUN A SANDY ON ME - To mislead by trickery, bluff.

GO SAND YOUR TONGUE - Stop, you're talking too much.

HE'S COLD OUT HEADED FOR JAIL - For certain, actually, really.

A ROUGH OLD COON - Hardbitten or aggressive old man.

TALK TO YOUR PLATE - To say grace.

MOUTH LIKE AN OPEN MAIL BOX.

WE NEED A GOOD THUNDER-GUST - Rainstorm, lightning.

ROLLIN' BOIL MAD - Very mad.

SOUTHERN SAYIN'S

LOOKS LIKE YOU WASHED IN A MUD PUDDLE AND COMBED YOUR HAIR WITH A TOWEL - Sloppy.

GO STICK YOUR HEAD IN A PIGGIN' - A small wooden bucket or churn.

WHAT GOOGERY-BOOGERY ARE YOU UP TO - Deceit, sometimes secret doings.

THAT FELLER IS COUNTRY SMART - One who becomes successful in the city.

SINGS LIKE A BELLYACHED HAWG.

PEART AS A MOUNTAIN BOOMER - Lively as a squirrel.

LOST HIS ROEBUCKS DOWN THE WELL - False teeth; in old times sold by a mail order firm.

DON'T NEED YOUR KNOWIN' STREWED OVER ME - Knowledge, book learning.

SOUTHERN SAYIN'S

HE LAID A SUGAR-MOUTH SPEECH ON 'EM - Honied, flattering.

TAKE THE RAG OFF'N THE BUSH - An expression of astonishment.

GATOR SWEAT - Liquor.

PEEL OFF - Leave, beat it, go.

RUN ONE'S MOUTH - Talks too much.

UGLY AS A MUD FENCE.

BUSY AS A LONG-NOSED WEEVIL IN A COTTON PATCH.

BACK-JAWED BACK SIDE-FRONT - Talked back with every remark.

COLD AS A WITCHES' TIT.

THET'S SORTA SLANTINDICULAR - Denotes slanting, also ANTIGODLIN, SKEWGEE and KITTYCORNERED.

SOUTHERN SAYIN'S

SO HUNGRY MY BELLY THINKS MY THROAT'S CUT.

WATER'S SO LOW THE GARFISHES ARE GETTIN' FRECKLE-FACED.

GOES AROUND LIKE AN ADDLED GOOSE - Crazy.

SHE STARCHED AND IRONED HIS HEAD - Lectured, bad-mouthed, tongue-lashed.

SUCH A NOISE YOU CAN'T HEAR YOUR EARS - Hard to hear.

A HURTIN' - In bad shape financially.

HE COULD RAISE RABBITS IN HIS BEARD - A heavy beard.

BAT-BRAINED - Crazy, foolish.

SINGS OUT HIGH NOTES LIKE HER FOOT IS CAUGHT IN A BAR (bear) TRAP.

SOUTHERN SAYIN'S

RABBIT TWISTER; HILLBILLY; RIDGE-RUNNER; GULLY-JUMPER; HAW-EATER; SORGHUM-LAPPER; FLINT-BUSTER; ELLUM-PEELER - All are derisive names given to backwoodsmen.

TOUGH AS WHITE (whit) LEATHER.

A CROW BIRD FOR CORN - Fond of boiled corn, not corn liquor.

COLD AS KRAUT.

SHE HAD HIM OVER - To reprimand, castigate or complain.

LAUGH, I ALMOST POPPED MY GIZZARD STRING - A supposed tendon in the stomach.

I'M A DONE TALK MAN - Finished talking, nothing more.

HE'S A SWAMP RAMUS - In Mississippi poor whites are/were called rednecks, peckerwoods or ramuses.

WOOL HAT BOYS - Small farmers; tenant farmers; sharecroppers. Called FLOPHATS in Louisiana.

ALWAYS PIROOTING AROUND - To root or nose around.

SOUTHERN SAYIN'S

I WAS IN AN UNSIGHTED ACCIDENT - Unforeseen, unexpected.

WE FOLKS OF THE UPBRUSH RELISH SINGING - Backwoods, hill country.

THEY GOT INTO A UPSCUDDLE - A quarrel.

HE'S JUST A SHIRT-TAIL BOY - Young boy.

HE THINKS HIS MOUTH IS A PRAYERBOOK.

DON'T GIVE ME THAT GATOR TAIL - A long drawn-out story, explanation, excuse.

GET GOING AND STOP YOUR POLLY-FOXING - To dilly-dally, delay and discuss.

HAS A TONGUE FOR TOLLING - To lure, lead on, entice with lies.

CAN TALK UP A TOW SACK - To fill a sack with foolish talk or nonsense.

SOUTHERN SAYIN'S

GUESS THAT'S ABOUT THE RIGHT SLAUNCH - An angle, usually sawed by guess rather than measurement.

HAVE SOME OLD NED - Fat pork, home cured bacon.

SECH AN ONSET YOU NEVER SEED - A fight.

JUST UP AND SHELLED OUT - Ran off very suddenly.

GUTS OF A BUTTERFLY - Timid, weak.

GOT A HEARING - A written reply to a letter.

A LINT HEAD - Cotton worker, usually a black person.

HE WAS HAMPERED IN GREENVAL - Jailed.

HE CAN'T MAN A SHOE BOX FULL OF GOOSE DOWN - Move about the soft, fine feathers of a goose.

FELL INTO MAGNOLIA - Lucky, inherited, fortunate.

TO LAY OUT - To not show up, loaf on the job, stay away.

HE KNOCKED THE TIDWADS OUTTEN HIM - Beat him, the stuffings.

LAND SO RICH SEEDS REFUSE TO LEAVE IT - Refuse to grow, said in jest about poor land.

THET TAKES THE HUCKLEBERRY OFF THE BUSH - Surprising.

HE'D CLIMB A RAINBOW FOR MONEY.

DOESN'T KNOW BEANS WHEN THE BAG'S OPEN - Stupid.

HE WAS NEVER WARRANTED - To be arrested on a warrant.

HE CAN RAISE HOGS TO WHO-LAID-THE CHUNK - Expression of approval, good, perfection.

HE'S GOT A RIG - A still, moonshine-making equipment.

HAVE YOU ANY COTTON REMBLINGS - Remnants.

THERE'S A LOT OF MOCKERS 'ROUND HERE - Mockingbirds.

HE WAS HANDSOME IN TIME - At one time, once.

HE'S OVER BY THAT SLICKSIDE - A large sloping rock.

SWAMP DEW - Moonshine, corn whiskey.

IN A SWIVET - Hurry, flutter, quandary.

HE CAN RUN LIKE A STREAK OF SUN-SHINE - Ability, fast.

DIDN'T BOLT MY EYES ALL NIGHT - To close one's eye or eyes.

SHE'S A KNEE-WEAKNER - Attractive girl.

GITS 'ROUND SO MUCH SHE KEEPS RUNNIN' INTER HERSE'F - Gossip, busybody.

HE FEATHERED INTO THE DUCKS - Shot into.

START ACTIN' HIGH-KAFLUTIN' - To put on airs.

WALKIN' IN/ON THE WIND - Head in the clouds.

SOUTHERN SAYIN'S

HE CAN CRUNCH PICAWNS 'TWEEN HIS BARE TOES - A strong man, bully.

SHE'S ALWAYS FLYING-UP-THE-CREEK - One who is flighty, upset.

STOP THAT, OR I'LL CLEAN YOUR PLOW - Punishment warning to unruly children.

EXCUSIN' GAWD, NOBODY KNOWS WHAT'S AHEAD!

COME ON DOWN FROM THE WALL - Get down to facts, be natural.

SO GANK-GUTTED HE CAN RUN BETWEEN RAIN DROPS - Skinny.

TOOK A SNIT - Crying fit, tantrum.

SALTED HIS BOTTOM - Shot in the rear with rock salt or buckshot.

IT'S COMING GREENUP - Springtime.

SOUTHERN SAYIN'S

TO MAKE A FANCY - To make a good impression.

FACE LIKE A TOW SACK OF TURNIPS - Bags under the eyes, jowels.

IN THE MULLIGRUBS - Ill temper, blues, sulkiness.

FLEW THE KUP - departed, home, escape from jail.

SLICK AS A BABY'S BOTTOM.

UP TO HIS EARS IN HORNETS - Trouble.

LIES LIKE A RUG - A liar.

PUT THE RUG - To die, "Pappy's 'bout to put the rug.

CUT THE DUST - Take a drink.

SO MOKY YOU COULDN'T SEE - Foggy.

MONKEY RUM - Distilled syrup of sorghum cane.

I GOT THE MISERY - A pain or ache.

WHEN IT'S FRIED THE SAUSAGE MEAT WILL GO AWAY - Shrivel, lose weight.

SOUTHERN SAYIN'S

MEAN ENOUGH TO FIGHT A CIRCLE SAW-MILL - Mill using a large circular saw.

TO GROUND-HOG IT - Person or family who are forced to live in poor circumstances.

DON'T THROW UP/OFF ON ME - To make fun of, disparage.

SHE'S MIGHTY NOTIONED WHEN SHE'S SICK - Peevish, impulsive.

IT'S WETTIN' DOWN OUT - Raining.

RUNS AROUND LIKE A BUMFUZZLED CATCH DOG. - Like a confused dog used to round up cattle, sheep, hogs.

I WAS IN A LI'L OL' TIGHT - Difficulty, predicament.

SHE TOOK THE BIGGEST THROUGH AT THE CHURCH - Ungovernable shouting, ecstasy, bodily contortions.

SOUTHERN SAYIN'S

KICK THE CAT - angry, upset

ROUGH AS A COB.

BEAT HIM INTO DOLL RAGS.

A DUNGHILL GENTLEMAN - country man

PITIFUL AS HAM WITHOUT EGGS.

ALL BELT AND BUCKLE - fat, protruding belly

BITTER AS GAR BROTH - gar fish

WORTHLESS AS A DEAD 'POSSUM TAIL.

POOR AS A SNAKE.

BUMBLINGS - Adulterated whiskey.

HE BUSSED HER GOING HOME - He kissed her.

SHE HAS NOTHING 'CEPT CALAMATIES - Second-hand merchandise.

SHE'S AILISH - Sick.

SHE AIN'T MUCH THESE DAYS - Not very well, ill.

I ARKANSAWED THE KITCHEN - To sweep with a broom.

HE AZZLED OUT OF IT - Back out, to move backward.

AIN'T WORTH A BAUBLE - A trifle.

HE CAN STEAL THE HAT OFF YORE HAID, AN' YOU LOOKIN' AT HIM.

BIBBRIE or BIBEY - Liquor made from the palmetto.

SET, AN' GIT A-KNOWN - Sit down and get acquainted.

STAGGERED LIKE A STUCK HOG.

IT'S BUSTED TO FOMDERJIGS - All in pieces.

FULL OF MAD AN' CABBAGE - Boiling mad.

BOW UP IF YOU WANT TO HOLD YOUR JOB - Improve.

TELL IT WITH THE BARK ON - All the truth, facts.

SHAKES YOUR HAND LIKE A PUMP HANDLE.

PUT THE CAT ON ONE - To get the better of one.

DOESN'T KNOW "A" FROM "IZZARD" - Doesn't know what he's talking about.

GAVE HIM THUNDER AND LIGHTNING - Gave him a tongue-lashing.

RUNS 'ROUND LIKE A VOLLYDO - Merry-go-round.

RODE HARD AND PUT UP WET - Tired, worn out.

A DUNG-BEETLE MIND - Always changing.

ROUGH AS A PINDER SHELL - Really rough.

PIZZY-AZZED DRUNK - Drunk as you can get.

MAD AS WHIZ.

HE COULD MESS UP A CLOUD-BUST.

ARGUFY A STUMP - Argue with a tree stump.

AS FAIR AS YOUR HAND - Plain as day.

SORE AS A RISIN' - Boil or pimple.

MONEY THINKS I'M DEAD - Can't make any money.

HE SWAM INTO THEM - Got into the fray.

HOT 'NUFF TO ROAST THE DEVIL - Very hot weather.

ASKIN' FER THE BOX - Pine box, coffin, asking for trouble.

WAKE UP THE SNAKES, DAY'S A-BREAKING!

AH WASTED THET TEN DOLLARS - Spent it, (not squandered).

YOU'RE ALWAYS YARMIN' - Complaining.

HE'S ALWAYS RAISING SAND - To start a commotion.

WALKS AT A HORSE-MILL GAIT - Slow, but steady. Sometimes said "Walks at a snail's gallop."

GIVE THE CHILD HIS PLAY-PRETTY - Toy.

RUN A RIG ON HIM - To play a trick or joke on one.

PIEPRINT OF HIS DADDY - Likeness.

SOUTHERN SAYIN'S

ACTS AS SNEAKY AS A SHEEP-KILLIN' DOG - Said of a person.

HER TONGUE GOES LIKE A BELLCLAPPER - Talkative.

IF YOU YAWN, HE'LL STEAL THE CHAW OF TERBACCER OUTTEN YORE MOUTH.

I HAVE NO MORE IDEA THAN A SNAKE HAS FLEAS.

A HEART SOFT AS SUMMER BUTTER.

UGLY AS HOMEMADE SIN.

HE WAS CHURCHED FER CYARD-PLAYIN' - To put on trial before the church, to expel (one) from the congregation; discipline by church action.

UGLY AS SKUNK-CABBAGE.

FITS LIKE A HOG IN A SADDLE - Misfits.

FAT AS A 'SIMMON FED HOG - Persimmon.

SOUTHERN SAYIN'S

AS SURE AS EGGS.

CUT MY HEART STRINGS - Broke my heart.

HE WAS OLD WHEN NEW ORLEANS WAS A BLUEPRINT.

HAPPY AS A BEAR IN SOURWOOD - In honey.

OLDER THAN GOOD (gawd).

DOODLY SQUAT - Indifference.

CAVORTIN' 'ROUND LIKE A FAT PONY IN HIGH OATS - Said of a moneyed person.

AN ORGAN-PEALING VOICE - Loud, with with inflections.

HOMELY ENOUGH TO CURDLE MILK.

HOT AS A FLITTER (not fritter).

DRINKS LIKE HE'D HEIRED A DISTILLERY - Inherited.

CHEAP TO KEEP AS A PET CLAM - Said of a wife.

WATER THE PALM TREE (lily) - To urinate.

GIVE ME YOUR HORSEBACK OPINION - Casual opinion.

SOUTHERN SAYIN'S

BROWNKITTIES GOT HIM - bronchitis

THE LAND IS SO STEEP, ONE STEP OFFEN MY PORCH AND YOU'RE HALF WAY TO ATLANTA!

HER HEART'S AS BIG AS HER BEHIND.

SQUEAKS LIKE A RAIN-FROG - A person with high, raspy voice.

PUT YOUR BRAINS IN A JAYBIRD'S HEAD AND HE'D FLY BACKWARDS.

SHAKES YOUR HAND LIKE HE WAS CLUBBIN' A SNAKE.

LIFE IS SHORT AND FULL OF BLISTERS.

ADOPTS ANYTHING THAT COMES ALONG - To become ill easily, contracts.

SO WET LAS' SPRING, MAH SKIN SPROUTED WATER CRESSES!

SOUTHERN SAYIN'S

BEAT HIM INTO DOLL RAGS.

A DUNGHILL GENTLEMAN - country man

PITIFUL AS HAM WITHOUT EGGS.

ALL BELT AND BUCKLE - fat, protruding belly

BITTER AS GAR BROTH - gar fish

WORTHLESS AS A DEAD 'POSSUM TAIL.

POOR AS A SNAKE.

FROM CAN'T SEE TO CAN'T SEE - From dawn to dusk.

CANEBUCK - Intoxicating liquor.

SHE HAS PLENTY COOKIN' FIXIN'S - Kitchen utensils.

I CREELED MY KNEE (NECK, BACK) - To wrench.

HAND ME THE CUP TOWEL - Dish towel.

HE GOT THE LIVIN' DAYLIGHTS DISPLEASURED OUT OF HIM - To beat, knocked.

I NEED SOME EASIN-POWDER - Medicine that allays pain.

I'M JUST FUNNING - Joking.

BRING IN SOME LIGHTWOOD - Resinous pine or other wood, kindling.

BUSY AS A COON IN A ROASTIN' EAR PATCH.

ASKIN' FER THE ROPE - Trouble, hanging.

A PO' OLD HIPPOED WOMAN - Suffering from an imaginary ailment.

I HAVE A SORE GOOZLE - The throat.

SHE'S BILIN' UP A MESS OF CLOUDS - Getting upset, angry.

YOU'RE A CULL FROM NOTHING - The lowest kind of person, reject.

SHE AND HIM WAS LILTING IN THE PARLOR ROOM - Singing.

HE'S SURE A JOE-DARTER - An unsurpassed person or thing.

IT GRAVELED ME - Embarrass, humiliate.

THAT HOUM'S FULL OF SNAKES - Mudflats or swampy places that dry in summer.

SHE'S TOO IFFY TO SUIT ME - Uncertain.

HE LEVELED DOWN ON THE CIDER - Drink, to cause the level of a fluid to go down.

GIVE THE BABY HIS HAPPY - Toy.

IT GRAMYS ME TO MEET HIM - Upsets.

CLEAN AS A HOUND'S TOOTH.

MAD AS A WET HEN.

UGLY 'NOUGH TO VOMIT A BUZZARD.

DEADER'N FOUR O'CLOCK.

SOUTHERN SAYIN'S

AIRYFIED AS A PEACOCK - Vain in dress or behavior.

HAPPY AS A HEN WITH ONE CHICK.

A-GINNIN AROUND - Fiddling, dabbling, moving about.

BACKED OUT LIKE A SCARED SWIMP.

SNEEZE, YOUR BRAINS ARE DUSTY - You have said something dull or stupid.

MEAN AS A STRIPED SNAKE.

SWAMP SO DRY A MILLION BULLFROGS AIN'T NEVER LEARNED TO SWIM.

BUSY AS A BAREFOOT BOY IN AN ANT BED.

RATHER TELL A LIE ON CREDIT THAN THE TRUTH FOR CASH - Prefers to lie.

EXCUSIN' GAWD, EVERYTHING'S GOIN' TO HELL.

SOUTHERN SAYIN'S

I NEVER MET UP WITH SECH A SORRY FELLER - YOU GOT SOME SORRY LOOKIN' TIRES ON THET CAR - WHERE DID YOU GET THAT SORRY SUIT OF CLOTHES - Poor, worthless, most contemptible.

HE'S READY TO BE BORED FOR THE SIMPLES - Bored (or greased) for the simples (or hollerhorn or woobles) - Subjected to an imaginary operation or treatment as though to remove stupidity or insanity from the head; sometimes ironically said of a person in fun.

TOO WET TO PLOW - The end, to give up, all there is.

HAKED TO A FRANZY - Embarrassed, annoyed to distraction, madness.

GROWS A RIGHT SMART OF COTTON - A good amount.

I'M FEELING A RIGHT SMART BETTER - A great deal, much.

PUT THE BEE ON - To plague one.

RUN THE ROADS - Always on the road.

LIKE A HEN-WALLER-JOSTLE - Lively.

GOT WHAT THE BEAR GRABBED AT - Nothing.

TONGUE GOES ON LIKE A BELL CLAPPER.

UGLY AS HOME-MADE SOAP.

BUSY AS A BUMBLE BEE IN A BUCKET OF TAR.

MUGGY AS CLAM JUICE.

FLUFFIED LIKE A BLOSSOM - dressed up.

COLD AS A GRAVESTONE IN JANUARY.

EMPTY AS A JACKASS' HEAD.

HAS MORE WRINKLES THAN A WASHBOARD.

I'LL GO DRAW A BITE - Prepare a meal.

SHE WAS A CHUFFY GIRL - Short, stout.

SO WET THE OL' WOMAN WAS CATCHIN' CATFISH IN THE KITCHEN MOUSETRAP - A long period of wet weather.

THE LAND WAS SO STEEP YA COULD LOOK UP THE CHIMNEY TO SEE THE COWS COME HOME!

DON'T CONTRARY ME - Oppose.

HER BELLY WAS ALL POOCHED OUT - Swollen, distended.

ALL THE SIGNS NOTE UP FOR A HARD WINTER - Indicate.

A JAG OF TATERS - A small amount.

BUSY AS A BEE IN A BOTTLE.

SHE GOES KIYOODLIN' 'ROUND THE HOUSE - Singing joyously.

PERSISTENT AS A STARVIN' BEDBUG.

WE'RE GOING TO A SINGING - A gathering for a singing.

MARRIED 2 TIMES AND PAPPYED 23 - To beget, father.

SHE HAS A TIPPY-TIPPY WAY OF WALKING - Bouncy.

LOW DOWN AS A SNAKE - Low as you can get.

HE CAN CHAW CHUNKS OUT OF THE AIR - Mad.

TIGHT AS BARK TO A TREE - Stingy.

HARD AS A BOILED CANNON BALL.

YOU'VE GOT A GROUPER MOUTH - Large Southern fish, talkative.

A CUSTARD PUDDING PERSONALITY - Soft, weak, changeable.

SICK AS A DEAD HOG.

ALL COTTON AND CARAMEL - Sweetness and innocence.

TO OUTRUN GREASED LIGHTNING - Very fast, frightened.

PRETTY AS A SPECKLED PUP.

SICK AS A TROMPED-ON TOADY-FROG.

TIGHT AS DICK'S HATBAND.

RICH AS MUD - Poor.

GLUTTED TO THE GULLUCK - Intoxicated.

SOUTHERN SAYIN'S

YOU AIN'T GOT THE SENSE OF A PECKERWOOD WITH THE DIZZIES - A woodpecker with a dizzy spell.

TRY JUMPIN' DOWN YOUR THROAT AND GALLUPIN' YOUR INNERDS OUT - Get out of here fast!

THERE'S A PLAT-EYE IN THAT WOODS - An evil spirit.

BORN DOWIE, I GUESS - Doleful, sad.

HAWK-EYE THE TABLE; HAWKEYE THE MELLION PATCH - To carefully observe, to stand watch.

ALWAYS PICKIN' A CROW - Finding fault.

HE'S THE UNTELLIN'IST FELLER - Unpredictable, erratic.

GRANDPA USED TO CALL THEM TUCKYHOES - Virginians who lived east of the Blue Ridge Mountains.

SOUTHERN SAYIN'S

A GRIN WIDE AS A WATERMELON RIND.

IN MORE TROUBLE THAN HOLDIN' ONTO A BEAR'S TAIL.

EXCITED AS A BUG IN A TATER PATCH.

HIGH AS A GEORGIA PINE - intoxicated.

YOU'RE MIGHTY COME A-RIGHT - You're right, quite correct.

WE HAD A REAL RIPPIT - Noisy party.

I WENT TO BALDMORE WUNST AN' NIGH SULTERED TO DEATH - Swelter or stifle.

CAT-HEADS HARD AS BRICKS - Biscuits.

TAKE YOUR FOOT IN HAND AND COME - To walk, usually followed by and go, and come, etc.

HE GOT BOUNCED LIKE A BALL - Fired.

LIT UP LIKE ALADDIN - A lamp, intoxicated.

STEPPIN' HIGH LIKE A ROOSTER IN DEEP MUD - A person putting on airs.

FIRE IN HIS BELLY - Energy, lusty.

BRAINS OF A SAP-SUCKER - Bird.

THICK AS A TUB OF DRIED FLEAS.

DOWN IN THE BACK - Pains in the back.

LOOSE AS A GOOSE - Running of the bowels, diarrhea.

HIS HEAD'S SCREWED ON WRONG - Mixed up.

IN A TURKEY'S DREAM YOU CAN - Impossible, can't be done.

CROSS AS A SORE-TAILED BEAR.

BELLY TIGHT ENOUGH TO CRACK A TICK ON - Said after eating a large meal.

SHAKES LIKE A PAIR OF DICE.

PRETTY AS A GOGGLE-EYED PERCH - Real pretty.

WE TRIED TO ENJOY THEM - Tried to entertain them.

YANKEE WOIDS THAT `BREAK-UP´ SOUTHERNERS

UMBRELLER — umbrella
VANILLAR — vanilla
HOTEL PLAZAR — Hotel Plaza
ANTENNAR — antenna
ENCYCLOPAEDIA BRITANNICAR —
 Encyclopaedia Britannica
MELODRAMAR — melodrama
FLORIDY — Florida
DINER — Dinah
DILEMMAR — dilemma
SAWR — saw
IDEAR — idea
BERMUDAR — Bermuda
DRAWERING — drawing
POTTY - PATTY — party
DEM - them
DOIT — dirt
CUBER, CUBY — Cuba
KEYRECT — correct
KAGG — keg
AMERIKER — America
AY-RABB — Arab
AHSKED — asked
AVENOO — avenue, i.e. Brooklyn
AVENYUH — avenue, i.e. Fifth Avenyuh
MOITLE — Myrtle
BERLD — boiled, i.e. I like berled haigs.
BERCOTT — boycott
BUNK — bump, i.e. I bunked into him.
BOIGLAR — burglar
BOOTCHER — butcher
CARM — calm, i.e. carm and collected.
SOITAINLY — certainly
CHAMPEEN — champion
CHAUNCE — chance
CHINAR — China
COMMOICIALS — commercials
CONSOINED — concerned
DOZE — those
EMMA — Emmer

YANKEE WOIDS THAT BREAK-UP' SOUTHERNERS

EMPIRE — umpire, i.e. Shoot de empire!
INGINE — engine
GOIL — girl
POIL — pearl
T'OID — third
HAHNSUM — handsome
LAWR — law
NAISE — noise
ERL — oil
AINTMENT — ointment
ERSTER — oyster
NOOSPAPAH — newspaper
PACK — park, i.e. Pack the car!
PAWK — park, i.e. Brooklyn and de old pawk ain't da same.
PASNUP — parsnip
POISONALITY — personality (Bronx)
RAIL — real, i.e. A rail chip off the old block.
RUFF — roof
RUBBAGE — rubbish
STOOD — stayed, i.e. I should'a stood at home.
NUTTIN' — nothing, i.e. He don't know nuttin'.
DEY — there, i.e. Dey ain't no fun in goin' to da zoo.
T'OUGHT — thought
T'INKIN' — thinking (Brooklynese)
POIPLE — purple
BOID — bird
COIB — curb
COIL — curl
WIT — with
DIS — this
DISHERE — this here
TRIBLE — triple
V'YAGE — voyage
WOIDS — words (Brooklynese)
YOUSE — Youse guys are nuts!
CHAS — I want chas to report ever' day!
PENSCOLER — Pensacola